W9-BMB-886

ALL WE HAVE IS ALL WE NEED

All We Have
Is All We Need

DAILY STEPS TOWARD

A PEACEFUL LIFE

Karen Casey

CONARI PRESS

First published in 2006 by Conari Press,
an imprint of Red Wheel/Weiser, LLC
York Beach, ME
With offices at:
500 Third Street, Suite 230
San Francisco, CA 94107
www.redwheelweiser.com

Copyright © 2006 Karen Casey. All rights reserved. No part of this
publication may be reproduced or transmitted in any form or by any means,
electronic or mechanical, including photocopying, recording, or by any
information storage and retrieval system, without permission in writing
from Red Wheel/Weiser, LLC. Reviewers may quote brief passages.

Library of Congress Cataloging-in-Publication Data
Casey, Karen.
 All we have is all we need : daily steps toward a peaceful life / Karen Casey.
    p. cm.
 ISBN 1-57324-268-3 (alk. paper)
 1. Meditations. I. Title.
 BL624.2.C365 2006
 204'.4—dc22

                                                        2005033554

Typeset in Perpetua by Gopa & Ted2, Inc.
Printed in Canada
TCP

13 12 11 10 09 08 0 7 06
8 7 6 5 4 3 2 1

Contents

. . . ─────────────────────────────

Introduction

$\cdots$

THESE DAYS, our lives can feel so hectic and out of control, so lacking in hope and joy. And yet every day, opportunities to experience joy and create peace-filled lives come our way. We have within us the enormous potential to *create peace*.

It's a matter of how we view the people and experiences in our lives. Being willing to see things differently is all that we need. Every time we respond to a situation with love rather than anger, or fear, or hatred, we take a step toward a more peaceful life, and each step creates its own momentum for positive change—small changes that ripple their way ever outward, influencing other people, other communities, and, ultimately, the world.

That's right. Your decision to act from a place of love contributes to the well-being of all humankind. No matter how crazy the rest of the world seems, we are neither helpless nor hopeless. And the power to effect peaceful change is as close as our next thought. We have within us all we need to do our part in making this a more peaceful world. I'm not just playing with words when I say, *all we have is all we need.*

All we need to do is shift our own perspective, and we can create the very miracles we seek. The world we see and experience is nothing more or less than a reflection of us, every one of us, and the way toward peace comes through such simple actions as responding with love to our spouse or child, behaving with courtesy toward the person sitting next to us in a meeting or on the bus, smiling at the person standing ahead of us in line at the grocery store. We offer nourishment to all of us every time we say a silent prayer for someone. It's all about what we send out from our hearts.

Perhaps you have heard this before. Even if you have, I believe you will find much value in the thoughts I share with you in the pages that follow. We often need to hear about an idea several times before we are willing to try it on for size. Here I give you lots of ideas to choose from.

It's important to remember, however, that it's not our job to change anyone else. Our job is to practice new behaviors. How lucky we are that we can do this. We can serve as the change agents that our families and communities need, that *we* need.

Let's not shy away from our responsibility. Instead, let's be grateful for the many opportunities to express more peace-filled lives that come our way every day. It's through our example that others will be inspired. Then and only then will we see the change that Margaret Mead expressed so long ago when she said, so eloquently, "Never doubt that a small group of thoughtful, committed people can change the world. Indeed, it's the only thing that ever has."

How to Use This Book

This book offers ideas for baby steps we can take every day that will add up to a peaceful life and a peaceful presence in the lives of others. The daily thoughts are grouped into six parts, each dealing with a different aspect of the process.

I designed the book so that it can be opened to any page for inspiration. You don't need to read it front to back. You can, of course, read it all the way through, returning to those thoughts that are most meaningful for you. Or you can start with the part that speaks to you right now and work with those ideas, or open to any page at random and see what's there. Read one thought each morning for inspiration, or read several and select the ones that you need to practice today. You may want to write down the ideas that you would like to remember and post them around your home, car, or office where you are most likely to see them. Or tuck this small book into your pocket or briefcase or purse and read a few passages when you have a free moment during the day.

Throughout these pages I refer to God or to a Higher Power as my partner on this path. When reflecting on the thoughts presented here and bringing them into your own life, you may prefer to use another phrase— Creator, the Divine, the Universe—that encompasses a universal life force as you understand it. The word or phrase used isn't important—what *is* important is your willingness to take steps forward, every day.

So go ahead. Take one step toward a more peaceful life, and then another, and another. Creating peace is not about making sudden, big changes, but about the accumulation of many tiny changes. And it starts with us. But watch out! Once you start down this road to peace, life will never be the same.

Honor Our Common Path I

· · ·

DEVELOPING A WILLINGNESS TO LEARN, FORGIVE,
AND MAKE AMENDS IN OUR RELATIONSHIPS

THE MEN AND WOMEN who share our journey
today, along with those who shared it yesterday
and those who will come calling tomorrow, do not make
their appearances coincidentally. We share this path by
design, because of the lessons we need to learn from one
another. We have on some level selected one another, and
it's within these carefully selected relationships that the
lessons we need to learn present themselves. The people
we meet today are our teachers.

And we switch roles, moment by moment. In one
instance we may be the teacher, and in the next the student. The dance is what matters.

That doesn't make every experience easy, however.
Some lessons are very difficult, in fact. But, usually, the
difficulty lies in our resistance to embracing the lesson,

to seeing the experience as hopeful or beneficial or spiritual or necessary to the growth we are ready to enjoy. And our resistance usually invites resistance from our teacher, too. It is helpful to remember that our Higher Power is part of the equation.

Being in the role of teacher or student in all our relationships is the constant in our lives. That's the exciting news, and it makes all interactions purposeful. We may choose not to appreciate the purpose or learn the lesson that's calling to us, and that's okay. A similar experience, with a similar lesson, will come our way at another time. We are not being held to a specific timeframe. We are held only to the lessons. When we learn them is up to us.

The ultimate lesson, of course, is forgiveness. Forgiveness of ourselves and of one another. And we can best accomplish this through making amends when we have harmed ourselves or others. The healing that fills our hearts and the hearts of our companions on this path when we make an amend is the substance that allows each one of us to carry the message of hope and love to all the people we meet on a daily basis. No one heals in isolation. Every opportunity we take to extend ourselves to others in a forgiving way heals hearts. And never just one. . .

The simple but powerful ideas in this part of the book will help you, one day at a time, to look carefully at your relationships, approaching them more lovingly or openly or honestly, with full awareness that they are exactly the relationships you need in order to grow into the person you are meant to be. A particular relationship may not seems like a blessing when we're in the midst of an argument, but if we remember that all arguments are masking fear and that a loving response is always the right response, we can incorporate the experience into our journey in a way that makes our "trip" what it is supposed to be.

Let's not waste any more time. Let's look at every person and every experience throughout the day with the joy and gratitude that they deserve. Without these people, without these experiences, we would not be capable of doing the work we have been called here to do. No one of us is without purpose, just as no experience is without purpose. We must do our part toward making this world a more peaceful place; each person we meet is an opportunity that's been divinely sent to us for extending the love that is necessary to heal our personal lives, our communities, and the world beyond us too.

Only one person has to be kind for a
relationship or situation to dramatically change.
I will be kind today.

. . . . .

We will not hear the messages we need to
hear if we isolate ourselves from the
message carriers.
I will join with others today and trust
in the process of life.

. . . . .

Listening is a tool that will help heal
our relationships. I can make the commitment
to *listen* today.

We are helping or hindering ourselves
and one another each time we speak.
I will remember this today.

. . . . .

Our relationship to the world community is
helped by our willingness to listen to the
travelers on our path. I will pay
attention to them.

. . . . .

Difficult relationships generally have the most
to teach us. Am I willing to learn?

. . . . .

We need the people who are sharing our journey,
all of them. They have much to teach us, and we
them. Do I show up for the lessons?

Each lesson needs our acceptance so that we can offer our insights to another person who is journeying with us. We are constantly students and teachers. I will likely be both today.

. . . . .

The primary lesson in this life is to forgive ourselves and one another. I can release any grudge or resentment I may be holding on to. I will begin by developing the willingness to forgive today.

. . . . .

All struggles, big and small, allow us to give and receive forgiveness.

Being willing to resolve any conflict contributes
to world peace. I can do my part today by
making a small decision.

. . . . .

Experiencing one peaceful relationship will
change every experience one has.

. . . . .

There is really only one relationship to heal.
Am I showing up lovingly?

. . . . .

When we commit to healing one relationship,
all relationships benefit. Am I willing to
change my behavior today?

Changing our behavior in one relationship
makes it easier to change it in all relationships.
Can I take the first step today?

. . . . .

Our judgment of others holds us hostage while
it harms those we judge. Am I willing to
give up my judgments today?

. . . . .

Our growth in relationships depends on our
willingness to love and forgive. Sitting in
judgment prevents both. Is there someone
I should forgive today?

The travelers on our path are exactly where
they are supposed to be. The same is true for us.
Am I willing to appreciate this fact today?

. . . . .

Every person we meet has been chosen to share
our path. Our willingness to cherish this idea
gives all our encounters the meaning they
deserve. Am I seeking the opportunity
for growth that is present within
every experience?

. . . . .

Each time any one of us remembers that God
is always present, we help those individuals who
are not, in that moment, remembering.
I am willing to do my part in helping
others remember today.

Never lament what appears to be a failed
relationship. Every relationship has played a part
in our journey. Am I grateful for this
understanding today?

. . . . .

Being courteous makes us feel good,
just as it pleases those who are sharing
our journey today.

. . . . .

Relationships allow us to heal.
Isolation prevents our healing.
Am I making healthy choices today?

. . . . .

Our isolation harms the people who need us on
their journey at the same time that it's harming us.
Am I willing to reach out today?

Being in a relationship with others is why we are
on this journey. Don't resist the opportunities
to grow that present themselves today.

. . . . .

There is no discussion that cannot be helped by
the remembrance that God is present at the
discussion too. Be alert to God today.

. . . . .

Resentments clearly injure us. And others.
Our relationships are intentional.
Ask, "What do I need to see today?
Is there an amend that needs
to be made?"

Forgiveness heals, ourselves and others too.
Am I willing to forgive a friend
or perhaps a stranger today?

. . . . .

We cannot feel resentment and forgiveness at
the same time. The choice is obvious.

. . . . .

Regardless of any painful experience, it must
finally be forgiven if we are to know peace
in all our relationships. Am I willing
to consider this possibility today?

. . . . .

The accumulation of unforgiven resentments
becomes "the stuff" of wars.
Ask, "Am I contributing to peace today?"

The greatest deed for humankind we can
contribute today is forgiveness. Do I need
to seek an opportunity to forgive
a past hurt today?

. . . . .

Forgiveness honors others. It softens us, too.
I may have an opportunity to help two
or more people today. Will I take it?

. . . . .

Be grateful for every relationship. It has come
our way by design. Even those relationships
we are not peaceful in have something to
offer us if we change how we see them.
Am I looking?

Seemingly insignificant relationships are
as important as the very memorable ones.
Believing this will change every
experience in one's life.

. . . . .

Difficult relationships educate us. We need
them. We can walk away, and the lesson they are
offering will come in another way, on another
day. The decision to stay is ours. Today may be
the day for making this decision.

. . . . .

Remember that "who you see is who you are" in
the moment of seeing. Understanding this can
change the complexion of every relationship.
Am I seeing what I want to see today?

Our relationships teach us everything we have
come here to learn. Are you taking advantage
of your opportunities today?

. . . . .

Relationships teach us how to forgive. They also
present opportunities for making amends.
Our hearts are softened by both. That's why
they are significant. Do I need to do one
or the other today?

. . . . .

We cannot learn how forgiveness feels in
isolation. And forgiveness is what ushers peace
into our lives and into the lives of those we
journey with, both here and elsewhere.

Isolation never, ever solves a problem. It will however, complicate it. I will focus my energy on being present to my teachers today. My solution will be found there.

. . . . .

Every relationship is connected to every other relationship one has. None are inviolate. Can I honor this idea today by how I treat every person I encounter?

. . . . .

To do no harm is a shortcut to improving all relationships. Making this choice even once today will have a positive influence.

Doing no harm in one relationship
miraculously improves all relationships.
Experience this miracle today.

. . . . .

Every person who refrains from harming
someone today improves the relationships
of every other person today.

. . . . .

The choice to do no harm is the least
complicated choice to make today.

. . . . .

Any discomfort tells us that we have work to
do in our relationships. Maybe it's time
to make an amend. I am willing to
consider this possibility today.

Being in relationships with others is why we
are here. Am I fully appreciative
of this information today?

. . . . .

What you give in one relationship, you give in
all relationships. Today is no exception.

Take the Road to Peace II

LETTING GO, SURRENDERING THE NEED TO
CONTROL, AND ACCEPTING WHAT IS

THE DESIRE to control our loved ones and the events in our lives is seductive, very powerful, and so very foolish. We are all guilty of trying to control other people, but we will never find peace by making a hostage of someone. The men and women in our lives are there for only one purpose: they are our preselected teachers. Every interaction is divine. Every encounter is intentional.

Surrendering our attempts to be in charge of other people or events relieves us of a huge burden. It may seem like there is too little to do if we're not trying to make others do our will. Trying to manage everything has become our job. But being in charge of our own behaviors and attitudes is a full-time job, and it's the only one we need! We will eventually love the freedom that we feel if we give up the illusion of control. We never really had it anyway. We only thought we did.

Letting others live their own lives takes willingness coupled with practice. One of the gifts of letting go of control over other people's lives is that it gives us the time to attend to our own needs and decisions. In the process, we discover that we have very rich lives that are quite separate from our loved ones', lives that are full of joy and promise. When we focus on the details of other people's lives, we're not able to see the opportunities for new experiences that have been trying to get our attention all along. Lucky for us, they've waited, and they will continue to do so until we are ready to notice them.

Alongside of giving up control over people and experiences is acceptance of the people and events in our lives as they are. Careful attention will reveal that every conversation, every event, has a message for us and every person has a part to play in the drama that's unfolding in our lives. We don't have to understand why an experience has captured our attention or why a particular person has come calling. It's appropriate to celebrate the importance of our interactions no matter where they happen; they are the experiences that carry us to the next stage of our education. In many instances of conflict with our companions, we—and the relationship—will be best served if we remain quiet. Or perhaps simply smile rather than turn away. The practice of accepting what has arisen as an opportunity for growth and then letting go of any desire to control it is the right response. Surrendering to a situation where necessary, and letting God be in charge of all people and outcomes, will make all our relationships more fun and more peaceful. We do get what we need. Just not always what we want.

Our entire perspective on life, on one another and on why we are here begins to change when we release our grip on the people and the outcomes that are hovering around our experiences. Take a deep breath, and *let go*. And let the messages that follow on the next few pages guide your daily affairs. Each message suggests a simple task. The effect can be quite profound, however.

Detachment is not indifference. And it doesn't
mean we don't love and respect someone.
On the contrary, it is a true expression of love.
Today, my experiences will be opportunities
for expressing detachment.

. . . . .

To understand acceptance, when you are
experiencing a struggle, change places with the
other person for a moment. How does this feel
in your heart? Practice this exercise today.

. . . . .

The freedom of saying nothing rather than
something hurtful is empowering.
Try it today.

Do you want to discover the solution to your
problem today? Surrender your grasp on it,
and wait for your answer.

. . . . .

How we see everyone on our path is a choice.
Praying for the "kinder vision" makes acceptance
a reality. Today offers us an opportunity
to practice this.

. . . . .

Every conversation we have is intentional.
Let's listen closely today and accept
the message.

Don't shy away from any person. His or her
presence here is by design. At the end of the day,
take note of what you learned.

. . . . .

Those people who seem to appear in our lives
again and again are being drawn to us.
Let's be grateful for their presence and
our need for one another. Do you wonder
what the lesson is?

. . . . .

The people we need for the lessons we are ready
for will follow us until we surrender to
the lesson. Maybe we should grow
into acceptance today.

Surrendering to the experiences that have been
hand-picked for our growth makes the journey
easier, more hopeful, and more peaceful.
Today is a chance to practice this.

. . . . .

There is no struggle too big to relinquish today.

. . . . .

Not having to win an argument is huge.
Why not experience this today?

. . . . .

Being the first one to back away from a conflict
sets a wonderful example. Today could prove
to be very peaceful.

Demonstrating for others that opinions can be
relinquished is a worthy action. Can I give up
an argument today?

. . . . .

Each time we walk away from a conflict,
we make walking away the next time easier.
I will no doubt have an opportunity
to do this today.

. . . . .

Gentleness lowers one's anxiety while it raises
the possibility for resolution to whatever is
causing one's tension. I can develop this by
breathing deeply before speaking today.

Being humble means being willing to accept
our shortcomings and then learn from them.
I will have an opportunity to practice
humility today.

. . . . .

Loving detachment releases all of us. It is the
easiest method of discovering peace too.
Today is certain to offer an opportunity
to practice this.

. . . . .

Truly letting go of one person teaches us how
easy it is to let go of other people too.
"Let go" will be my mantra today.

Seeing the good in a situation is little more than
a decision. But it's a decision that needs to be
made every day. Today is a beginning.

. . . . .

God is forever among us. Does that realization
inform your decisions? It should. Practice
remembering God today.

. . . . .

If you are feeling negative about a situation,
you can choose to remain quiet.
It's very empowering, in fact,
to make this choice. Try it.

Making the choice to surrender rather than
fight changes more than just ourselves.
One resolution benefits many struggles.
I will be a peacemaker today.

· · · · ·

Not engaging in arguments is very freeing.
Every day that we avoid an argument is a day
that's more peace-filled for everyone we meet.
I can add to the peace of the world today.

· · · · ·

Each time we walk away from an argument,
we feel greater empowerment. And then we
can walk away more easily the next time.

Our combined lessons, yours and mine, are like
the fingers of a clasped hand. Let's help one
another grow today. Our behavior will
make the difference.

. . . . .

The wisdom to remain quiet rather than
engaging in conflict will reap many benefits and
foster inner peace for all concerned.

. . . . .

No disagreement requires resolution. Ever.
Accepting our differences is the way
to peaceful lives.

We cannot escape our destiny.
Thank God!
Today I will remember to be grateful for
every aspect of my journey.

. . . . .

We cannot control others. Our only job is to
control ourselves. Will I remember this today?

. . . . .

Conflicts need two or more participants to keep
them going. We need never be one of them.
Can I choose to walk away before a conflict
attracts my involvement today?

The decision to walk away from an argument
is easier with some practice. But any tiny
disagreement today is the place to begin.

. . . . .

There are no accidents. Depending on how
we choose to respond, conflicts can be
our opportunities for growth. What choice
will I make today?

. . . . .

Feelings cannot control us. We choose them.
We harbor them. We can let them go.

. . . . .

Our journeys are intentionally intertwined.
Am I conscious of this today?

We need not understand the journey. However,
we must accept it and trust that God is in
charge. Am I remembering to include
God in my plans today?

. . . . .

Understanding why someone is on our
"radar screen" isn't mandatory. Trusting that
their presence is by design will comfort us,
however. I will take note of the people
walking with me today.

. . . . .

Never regret any experience. Instead,
let it inform you. Am I learning what I need
to learn today?

Surrendering in a conflict doesn't mean losing
or being second best. It means we are
opting for peace today.

. . . . .

Every person benefits from one person's
willingness to surrender. Am I willing
to do my part to benefit others today?

. . . . .

Nobody ever really wins an argument.
Feelings are always hurt. I will refrain from
hurting anyone's feelings today.

Until one practices the act of walking away from
a tense situation, the rewards cannot be
realized. I will remember that practice
makes perfect today.

. . . . .

Nothing is ever gained from digging in our
heels. Do I make a practice of this?
Am I willing to give it up?

. . . . .

One's entire perspective on all experiences
begins to change as surrendering becomes more
natural. If this is an appealing idea to you,
begin practicing it today.

If every single human being walked away from an argument, just one time today, the entire universe would feel the shift. Are you willing to do your part today?

. . . . .

We honor another person when we let him or her make their own choices. Each one of us has a particular journey to make. I will go about the business of making only mine today.

. . . . .

Detaching from the difficulties of others may appear unkind, particularly if their circumstances trouble us, but we must focus on our own journey, no one else's. Today will allow me to practice this.

Detachment frees each one of us to learn what
we need to learn, do what we need to do, and
grow in the ways we need to grow. I can make
the decision to do the right thing today.

. . . . .

Attachment to others binds us; it cripples us,
in fact. No attachment is healthy. A question
I must ask each day is, "Am I holding
someone hostage?"

. . . . .

Each person's journey is unique. We must
refrain from interference. Setting an example is
the only advice we should offer. Can I remain
quiet when I need to today?

Being in charge of ourselves is a worthy and
full-time job. It makes it easier to let go of
others, knowing they have a full-time job too.
This will be my goal today.

. . . . .

Not being able to change others benefits us
in many ways. I will cherish the freedom
this gives me today.

. . . . .

Were we able to change others, our work would
never be done. Today will be manageable.
I have only me to control.

Walking away from a situation, letting go of
people who are not mine to control, assures me
I will do no harm today.

. . . . .

There is no struggle that demands
resolution today.

. . . . .

Today's experiences are hand-picked.

Choose Joy III

MAKING LOVING CHOICES, ACTING AS IF,
AND RELINQUISHING FEAR

JOY IS THE BY-PRODUCT of making thoughtful choices. Showing attention to someone else, friend or stranger, through something as simple as a quiet smile, creates an inner joy. When you offer a hand to an elderly person who is struggling to walk or gain her balance, both people are made joyful. Choosing to step away from an argument—not always an easy choice—opens the door to genuine joy too.

We feel good every time we make a kind remark rather than a mean-spirited one. And the next kind remark comes even more easily. Joy is never far behind when we are guided by kindness. Every day we are faced with multiple opportunities to make a positive difference in someone's life, and every time we extend ourselves, we spread more joy around. There is really no better action we can take on a daily basis than doing one thing that will inspire joy in the heart of someone else.

And we don't necessarily have to feel kind or like smiling or like lending a hand to someone in need to make the choice to do it. Fortunately, acting as if we feel the urge to be helpful is the next best thing to actually wanting to be helpful, and the results are the same. Other people are affected in a loving way by our treatment, and our own hearts are changed, too, which just might mean that acting as if won't be necessary all that often in the future.

Attaining joy can be far easier if we remember a few simple suggestions (quite possibly the same suggestions we heard from our mothers or our first-grade teachers). Be kind always. Say nothing if you can't say something nice. Listen to the voices who are calling to you; they definitely have messages you need to hear. Trust that you are in the right place to learn what is next on your list of necessary lessons right now. And remember that you don't have to do anything alone. God is always just a thought away.

Our choice to enjoy a different kind of life is always available to us. But fear all too often claims our attention, preventing us from seeing the opportunities for joy and peace and thanksgiving as they present themselves. Let's not forget that fear has only the power we give it. It lives only in our minds. It can't control us without our consent. It is not stronger than our willingness to let God be in charge. The choice is ours.

One day at a time, we can think differently, act differently, feel differently, and help others have a different experience. Enjoy these next few pages one day at a time, and watch how your interior spaces begin to change.

Kindness can be practiced until it becomes real.
Acting as if we are kind is the way
to strengthen our willingness
to make kindness a reality today.

. . . . .

Acting as if we feel kind is just as good as
honestly feeling kind to begin with. The first
step is making the decision to be kind today.

. . . . .

Fear can be put to rest today and every day
when we remember that we have been prepared
for whatever experience beckons.

The thought that God is with us this minute,
as we read these words, is powerful, isn't it?
Well, God is powerful. Let yourself be
at peace in this awareness today.

. . . . .

No lesson will harm us. We may not like it.
We may be afraid of it. But if we remember
who our partner is, today will be
experienced with peace.

. . . . .

Fear separates us from the very people who
are destined to be on our journey.
Remembering this today will change
every experience I have.

All struggles reflect fear. I want to be willing to
understand what I am afraid of today.

. . . . .

The development of all good traits requires
willingness, honesty, commitment,
and practice. Am I willing to begin
the process today?

. . . . .

Making the decision to judge no one is a choice,
the right choice if we want a more peaceful life.
Have I been making this decision?

Repeating good choices is smart. Freeing others
from our judgment is one of these. Can I
commit to this for this day only?

. . . . .

Not judging others becomes easier the more we
practice acceptance rather than judgment.
It's a simple change of mind we can make,
one day at a time. One person at a time.
I will begin now.

. . . . .

We feel free and good when we give up the
inclination to judge. Others can feel our
acceptance immediately.

Practice changing your mind when you are
feeling negative. It's not so very hard.
Replace the negative thought with
a fond memory for a moment, and feel
your heart change. Try this today.

. . . . .

No response is always better than an angry one.
This is a simple decision that I can make
throughout the day.

. . . . .

A genuine smile can often diffuse an ugly
situation, and most ugly situations
deserve to be quietly ignored.
Am I smiling enough?

A deep breath can alleviate fear, give us time
to make another choice, and change our
perspective on the situation, the person,
the moment. Am I breathing
deeply often enough?

. . . . .

Changing the world is not our job. Changing
our mind is. The choice to do so is calling to us
every day. Will I listen today?

. . . . .

Choice is all we have. But more important,
it's all we need. I will choose wisely today.

Each one of us is affected by every choice each
one of us makes. Remembering this will help
me think before making any choice today.

· · · · ·

Making the choice to be peaceful can be habit-
forming. What a comfort! I will make
the effort today.

· · · · ·

Worry is a choice. Never a necessity.
Should I monitor my choices
more carefully today?

It's a simple decision to walk away from
an argument. It's just not an easy decision
the first time we try it. Practice will convince
us of the benefits, however. I will walk
away if I am being drawn into
an ugly situation today.

. . . . .

Recognizing the fear behind an attack allows us
to feel compassion. We may want to attack
back, but we can make the better choice.
What will I choose today?

. . . . .

Fear is the opposite of love, but it is a cry
for love, nonetheless. Am I willing to recognize
this? Will I look for examples today?

Where fear is present, a feeling of being
separate from others is the root. I can join
"the circle" if that's my choice, and the fear
will dissipate. What will I do today?

. . . . .

Seeing our oneness lessens our fear. Believing
in our oneness is a decision. Today I can
be fearless if I choose.

. . . . .

Fear creates more fear. Love, its opposite,
creates more love. To which side am
I contributing today?

Attack thoughts are always fear based.
Do I need to inventory what I am afraid of?
Am I willing to trust that love is a worthy
substitute for fear? Today and every day?

. . . . .

Fear thoughts can be replaced by loving
thoughts with the assistance of my
Higher Power, who is waiting
in the wings for me every day.

. . . . .

We can be comforted by the knowledge that all
is as it should be and we have nothing to fear.
God is near.

Fear is the more prevalent expression one
observes in others. It invites us to express love
in return. I will look for opportunities
to express love today.

. . . . .

One's fear can be relieved by remembering
God's presence in all situations. Willingness
to remember is all it takes to change our lives.
Today is a good day to begin remembering.

. . . . .

Every fearful expression another person makes
is a cry for help that we can answer with
a loving response or a kind prayer.
My day will be bettered if I meet all
experiences with love.

Make no response to any situation today that wouldn't be pleasing to God. This does simplify our lives, doesn't it?

. . . . .

Shifting one's perspective is a choice that becomes easier with practice. Seeking help from the God of one's understanding makes this possible. I will be willing to see my experiences differently if I am troubled today.

. . . . .

One shift in perspective, away from conflict, is a beginning to a better life for every one of us. We are connected. What any one of us does affects all of us. Am I willing to do my part for peace?

How we move forward is up to us.
Likewise, staying stuck is also up to us.
Which will it be today?

. . . . .

We need have no fear. Every experience is part
of our education. And what we learn can and
should be shared with others, too. I may
have an opportunity to teach today.

. . . . .

The choice to acknowledge the blessing
of everyone on our path makes a difference
in how we experience every encounter.
It will make this day better for
everyone else, too.

Let's trust that everyone present in our lives
has a purpose today.

. . . . .

Any new behavior can become second nature
with enough practice. Today might be the
turning point in my life.

. . . . .

A tiny change by each of us exponentially
changes all of us. The question to be asked
every day is, "Am I doing my part to
create a better world?"

Making the decision to be courteous isn't really
very hard. It begins with willingness.
Do I have it today?

. . . . .

Some good decisions have to be remade often.
The decision to be courteous is one of these.
How willing am I today?

. . . . .

Giving up negative judgment will change every
experience one has. It happens by taking
advantage of one opportunity at a time.
Today will offer many opportunities.

Doing no harm can become an easy choice with very little practice. Why? Because peace feels so much better than agitation. Try it today.

Go with the Flow IV

LIFE IS CHANGE. Wishing we could avoid change is the same as wishing we were dead. Our fear, of course, is that change will leave us vulnerable, unable to handle the repercussions that might result from it. However, change happens when we are ready for it. Not before. And we have been prepared for it. Always.

We don't understand this fact about change because of our fear of the unknown. But we can lay this fear aside. Now. God is on the other side of it, waiting to reveal the lessons we are ready for, lessons that are sheltered within the relationships we have attracted. We will not experience any change or any lesson alone. We do and will always have the comfort of our Higher Power as we journey through our lessons and the changes they foster.

We must realize, however, that the lessons we need aren't always the ones we want to embrace. But by making the decision to trust God's infinite wisdom that we are being sent the lessons we need, we can accept them more easily. And it's a guarantee that God does have a better idea of what we need than we have. We can facilitate this understanding of God's infinite wisdom by making periodic gratitude lists. They are wonderful reminders of all we have learned, all we have been given within the myriad relationships that have called to us.

Our relationships are the training ground for our lessons and subsequent growth. And they are not showing up willy-nilly in our lives. We have selected these lessons and these relationships, although we might have forgotten our requests. That's a truly exciting realization. We are where we need to be, today and every day, interacting with exactly the right people for the growth we have been prepared for. What we take away from each interaction is up to us, and we may choose, the first time it's presented, to avoid the lesson we had—perhaps subconsciously—requested, but it will wait for us. What a relief. On another day, the opportunity will come calling again.

And perhaps we'll be ready for it then. If not, it v
patiently wait.

The perspective we choose, and we are always in control of that, is what makes the difference in how we
respond to the experiences that attract our attention and
offer us our lessons. The combination of perspective and
willingness will make the path we journey on smooth or
bumpy. The joy we feel, or the sadness, or anger, or dis-
couragement, are responses that we have full control
over. The power to be at peace and certain of our direction and purpose is within our grasp every minute. There
is great hope for us, every one of us. And in the expression of our hope, we show others they can have hope too.

In the days ahead, let's remember that every experience we have is an opportunity to give the gifts of love,
compassion, understanding, honesty, listening, joining,
oneness, humility, acceptance, courtesy, and peace. Being
on the giving end of any one of these is what assures us of
the opportunity to share in the gift too. Or we can refuse
"our assignment," withhold all of these, and live a very
pain-filled, narrow life. The choice is ours. Really, how
hard can it be to make the right one?

When we become willing to see a situation from
another person's perspective, we can discern
a change in their body language, along with a
change in our own. Let's become aware
of the changes today.

. . . . .

Ask yourself, on a daily basis, "Is my perception
of a situation more important than my peace
of mind? Or might I be willing to shift it
for the benefit of all?"

. . . . .

Seeing with one's heart makes changing
one's perceptions easier. Am I open
to change today?

Seek the willingness to let go of your own
perspective. Ask your Higher Power for help
today and watch your experiences change.

· · · · ·

Take note that one's perspective is related to
one's past, never the present moment. Let this
help you look at today with greater clarity.

· · · · ·

Feel the change in your attitude, your
demeanor, your state of mind as you let
your own perspective go. Today can be
as happy as you choose to make it.

Kindness is a habit. And we can exchange a bad habit for this one any moment we choose. Today will present some opportunities.

. . . . .

Being kind changes us beyond our wildest expectations. Try it to believe it.

. . . . .

Never disregard anyone you meet. Each person is part of your destiny. Accepting this can make every experience a comforting one. Practice believing this today.

. . . . .

All relationships were hand-picked by us for the lessons we have come here to learn. Doesn't this make them more exciting?

No "learning partner" has to be cherished for
the lesson they are presenting to be learned.
This takes the sting out of situations if we let it.

. . . . .

Any lesson can be refused "right now."
The lesson will wait for us.
That's the good news, in fact.

. . . . .

Lessons come, and then they come again.
Fret not if you miss them the first time they
come. Today might be the day you are
ready for one of them.

Every lesson is one we need for the next stage
of our lives. We have requested it, and it has
come. Pay attention to those lessons
that visit today.

. . . . .

There is no struggle that doesn't have an
inherent lesson. Let's not run from a struggle
today, but be grateful for what we have
the opportunity to learn.

. . . . .

All struggles are blessings in disguise.
Hindsight certainly gives us a chance to see
when this was true in the past. I will not
shy away from a struggle today but will
seek to see the blessing instead.

In any struggle, I have a chance to know myself better. Which, in turn, means I will know my traveling companions better too.

. . . . .

We can be gentle and still be heard. It's a matter of perception. In many cases, indeed, the gentle voice is the voice that's most easily heard.
I will seek to be gentle today.

. . . . .

It is only in relationship with others that we experience our lessons. I will be ready for them today and cherish my growth.

. . . . .

What we do to one we do to all. This makes the choice to be gentle all the more powerful.
I will adhere to gentleness today.

We are the example for one another that each
one of us needs. I will set a good example today.

. . . . .

Attempting to be honest is a great beginning to
changing our behavior. However, every attempt
is only as good as our followthrough. Am I being
as honest as I expect others to be?

. . . . .

Acknowledging the importance of all the
travelers on our path is a humbling experience.
Not one of them is there by accident.
Will I remember this today when I am inclined
to be angry about the traffic?

The demonstration of honest, humble behavior
is the "assignment." It's this behavior that allows
us to serve as good teachers to those who are
sharing our path. Am I willing to be
a good teacher today?

. . . . .

Every time we judge another person we are
judging ourselves. A simple shorthand for this:
"You spot it, you got it!" Do I need a shift
in perception occasionally?

. . . . .

Those people we unfairly judge don't show up
by chance on our path. From them we will
learn what is next in our "curriculum."
I can dread this fact or look to
these others eagerly today.

We have combined forces to learn and to teach.
Unfair judgment prevents both. Am I willing
to show up lovingly today?

. . . . .

Seeking the good in every experience ensures
that you will bring your better self into every
encounter. Lives change when we do this—ours
as well as those we journey with today.

. . . . .

Being grateful for even one thing will have
an impact on how we see our lives and
the world around us. Have I made
my gratitude list today?

Reread recent gratitude lists any day you feel
unfairly treated or scared. Every item on the list
has been a gift from God. And the gifts
will keep arriving.

· · · · ·

God is everywhere and in everybody.
Lovingly look around today.

· · · · ·

Every changed mind, every peaceful mind
adds to the changing of the world.
Are you positively influencing the
world around you?
Take the opportunity to do so today.

Being right is all a matter of perspective.
Am I willing to be peaceful instead, today?

· · · · ·

Having to be right only satisfies us for a while.
It's short-term gratification at best,
and it will not make us peaceful today.

· · · · ·

Each time we walk away from an explosive
situation we are setting a good example
for others. Am I willing to make this
a priority today?

No argument needs our input. Staying out
of one today is good for our souls and the
souls of those who are watching us.

. . . . .

Where two people are fearful, only one person
has to change for the situation to be different.
I will be free of fear today if I remember
God is my partner.

. . . . .

The fact that we do not need to remember that
God is present for God to *be* present is our
assurance that God is everywhere.
What awesome relief this can bring us today.

We had a hand in selecting the lessons we are experiencing today. Remembering this takes the sting out of the hard ones, doesn't it?

. . . . .

Our experiences are like the foundation of a home. There is a proper order to how they present themselves, and none can be skipped forever. Today's lessons are on "the blueprint."

. . . . .

We cannot refuse, forever, a lesson we need to learn. It will simply keep appearing until we accept it. Does some lesson seem to be shadowing you lately? Maybe today will be the day to accept it.

Our lessons will wait for us. They are patient.
Today might be the right day to say, "Okay."

. . . . .

We will repeat the past until we learn from it.
We are both comforted and chagrined by this
situation. But there is another choice.
We can decide to learn the lesson. Today
is a good day for learning.

. . . . .

Be peaceful. Life is perfect as it is. It's only our
perspective that might need to change.
Am I willing to shift my perspective today?

Remembering who we really are makes the
expression of love far easier. And remembering
that our companions have been intentionally
selected makes them easier to love too.
Let me prove this today.

. . . . .

Changing the contents of one's mind can happen
instantly. And any time we aren't happy with our
lives, the solution lies within us. Today might be
a day to practice this exercise.

. . . . .

Nothing needs to upset us ever again when
we utilize the power to change our minds.
This is the miracle of life. It's also a profound
responsibility. Am I ready to accept
this responsibility?

The empowerment that is realized as the result
of shifting one's perspective is awesome.
Practicing is all that's required today.

. . . . .

Wherever we are, whoever we are with,
is our opportunity to practice shifting our
perspective. The results are astounding.
Are you willing to experience this today?

. . . . .

Being willing to see differently is all that's
necessary for a different perspective to emerge.
This is a small decision and not a hard one
either. Practice it today.

Our lives will change dramatically if we become
willing to change our minds about how we see
our experiences and the people in them.

. . . . .

Each positive shift in perspective positively
changes the lives of our companions too.
See how this works today.

. . . . .

When enough people choose to shift their
negative perspectives, relationships around
the world will change. This may seem
impossible, but it's true. Are you willing
to do your part today?

Thoughts manufacture feelings. Are you willing
to change your thoughts so you can have
a peace-filled life today?

. . . . .

Our lives will not change unless we are willing
to exchange the thoughts that are keeping us
unhappy for thoughts that will make us joyful.
Today just might give you an opportunity
to make a new choice.

. . . . .

We repeat old patterns when we hang on to old
thoughts. Are outdated thoughts still ruling
your life? You can give one up today.

We need not continue to see how we
always saw. What a revelation!

. . . . .

Seeing as God sees is the assignment.
Have I been practicing this? Can I make
the effort today?

. . . . .

Fresh interpretations offer new understandings.
All it takes is willingness to be open to new
interpretations for them to be revealed.
I will be open today if a conflict
is on the horizon.

Growth depends on our willingness to see our
lives differently, with God's help. Today can
offer me a fresh perspective.

. . . . .

Nothing changes if nothing changes.
What a concept! I may need to be willing
to change my mind today.

. . . . .

Every person is holy. Remembering this
in every instance today will change the
complexion of every encounter.

Every conversation is intentional. Am I willing
to learn what is beckoning to me today?
That's the key to a changed life.

. . . . .

Every experience offers us a lesson we need.
If we remember this, it will change our
perspective on everything, and we
will know peace. Today can be
filled with hope.

. . . . .

Every person we meet with today has
volunteered for the lesson we are sharing.
What an awesome realization this is.

What I believe at any one moment in time isn't
necessarily the truth. But it does serve my needs
until additional information gives me a better
perspective. I will be open to a changed
perspective today.

. . . . .

We get the partners we need for the lessons we
have requested. There are no accidents in the
way our lives are unfolding. If I can appreciate
this today, I will be free from anxiety.

. . . . .

We will continue to meet the people we need
to meet on our journey. They are part
of our destiny. We may meet some
of them today.

We simply cannot avoid the lessons we need. If we aren't ready for them today, that's okay. They will come calling on another day, perhaps in another form, but they will come.

. . . . .

Courtesy can change every aspect of one's day. The decision to be courteous is a tiny one but ever so powerful. I will practice courtesy today.

. . . . .

Regard all people as your teachers and be grateful for them. At the grocery, in traffic, in the workplace; our teachers are everywhere. I pray to remember this today.

Detachment is the one lesson that is common to
all of us. We can help each other learn it today
by setting the example of practicing it.

. . . . .

The power of our decisions is awesome,
and we can remake our decisions when more
information is present. Today will
give me new information.

. . . . .

Growth requires interaction with others.
Of course we can avoid changing, but that's
to the detriment of everyone who shares
our journey. I will have many
opportunities to grow today.

Acknowledging that we are seeing ourselves in
the way we see others is the first step toward
our healing. Am I willing to learn
what I need to today?

. . . . .

Our perceptions of people and events change
with our willingness to look at them a second
and maybe a third time. Today will present
myriad opportunities for seeing anew.

. . . . .

The decision to change a perception can be
made instantaneously. Will I be willing to do this
today if a circumstance calls for it?

Changing one perception makes changing
a second perception far easier. Practicing any
exercise is advantageous. I am willing today
to change what needs changing.

. . . . .

My perceptions live in my mind only. Everyone
I meet has his or her own perceptions, too.
It's not my job to change anyone else's.
I will remember this today.

. . . . .

We have the capability of changing our lives
by changing our perceptions of the people
in our lives. Today will offer
some opportunities.

We have the opportunity to change our lives
and the lives of everyone who is on our path,
every time we change our perception
and see others rightly.

· · · · ·

Let's do our part to change how this world is
affecting all of us by changing how we see this
world around us. Let's begin today.

· · · · ·

Be glad for each lesson today. It resides in
our conversations with others.

Play Well with Others V

CHOOSING KINDNESS, CREATING PEACE, AND LIVING IN THE NOW

CHOOSING KINDNESS is a tiny decision that can be made while in the throes of any encounter. Being kind doesn't necessarily mean taking a particular action. For instance, we don't have to pay someone a compliment if we're not feeling supportive. Nor do we have to listen intently to a diatribe or agree with a companion when we honestly have a different opinion. Rather, we might simply interpret being kind in certain instances as not doing something that is unkind. None of us is confused about the difference between a kind act and one that's unkind.

Perhaps an even more important reason for being kind is that it enhances our own level of peace. And the more peaceful we are, the greater are the benefits we bring to the others who are sharing our journey. I've said before and it's worth saying again: We are on "assignment" here. Our lives are full of purpose and intent. Our mission is to spread more joy and hope and peace and forgiveness to the others we meet. And they, in turn, will be inspired to do likewise. It's surely not folly to try to achieve these goals in our own lives, in our families, and in our communities. We could be spending our efforts far more frivolously.

If feeling peaceful eludes you quite often, perhaps it's because you are trapped by the past or caught in anticipation of the future. Unless we are steeped in the moment, this exact moment, we will not enjoy the full benefits of peace. *Now* is where peace resides. Dragging the past forward means we are incapable of ever seeing the present. And fretting over what might be, or might never be, allows no room for the experience of this breath of fresh air. That's what we find *now:* a freshness that's unencumbered by what never really was anyway.

How simple life can actually be. Yet how very complicated our egos want to make it. This is not to say we should live in denial about the tragic circumstances that might be playing out somewhere in the world. But focusing on the tragedy doesn't alleviate it. Bringing a peaceful perspective to the situation changes how it looks and allows us to see how it might be resolved.

Living in the problem rather than the solution is what keeps so many of us stuck in old habits. Resistance to the possibilities that lie within the circle of hope and kindness and gentleness and peace keeps all of us from moving forward. Let's not forget that what stops any one of us stops all of us. Just as what we do to one, we do to all. Our interconnectedness, our oneness, is a fact of life. Perhaps it's not easy to understand. It's even harder to see. But we trust that it's so, and we will find it far easier to offer kindness and peacefulness and hopefulness wherever our journey takes us.

Every day of our lives we are blessed with opportunities to make a difference in someone's life. Let's not close our eyes to these opportunities. Let's be grateful that we have been called to make a difference. It means we are here by design and that our purpose is not yet fulfilled. By following any one of the simple suggestions on the next pages, we will bring goodness to our relationships, and the world will be a better place because of it.

A good habit to develop is to monitor our
thoughts prior to acting on them. It takes only
a second or two to do this, and the
payoff is immediate.

. . . . .

When in conversation today, quiet your own
mind completely. This response may not come
naturally, so be prepared to practice.

. . . . .

Focus intently on every word another person
is saying to you today. When your mind wanders
to your own thoughts, as it will, bring it back
ever so gently, so as not to miss the
message you need to hear.

Listen to everyone's words from your heart today. Note how that changes your perspective on them and the moment.

. . . . .

Feel the tension leave your body when you let your heart be your ears today.

. . . . .

Be grateful for the willingness to be at peace today. It's a decision we can make by controlling what we harbor in our minds.

Listening intently to the messengers on our
journey today fosters peace of mind when
we remember that our lessons lie
within their words.

. . . . .

Our response to the others who walk among us
is our gift to the moment, which eventually
touches all of us.

. . . . .

Choosing peace over winning an argument
is easier the second time we try it. Today
will give me an opportunity.

Our interactions are not coincidental. Neither
are our opportunities to be bearers of peace.
I pray to remember this all day.

. . . . .

This world needs every loving resolution it can
garner. Are you willing to be a contributor
for the good of us all today?

. . . . .

Being gentle doesn't mean being walked on.
Kindness comes in many forms.
Find a way to be kind today.

Using a quiet voice generally indicates gentleness. We can avoid unnecessary injury if we are both gentle and quiet. Seek an opportunity to be gentle today.

. . . . .

Gentle people often speak slowly. They want to be understood, and they want to nurture others by their words. Am I using a gentle voice today?

. . . . .

Responding to anger with gentleness changes the direction of the discussion while it changes both individuals. Making the choice to be gentle is a transforming experience. I will try it today.

To do nothing more than be gentle in every
interaction, for one day, will change one's life
completely. Why not try it today?

. . . . .

Being gentle in one instance makes being gentle
in the next instance even easier. Practice is what
changes us completely. Today is
a good day to begin.

. . . . .

Doing no harm doesn't necessarily mean doing
something different. It may mean doing
nothing, and that's quite okay.
Today will give me
many opportunities to do nothing.

If we are at peace with ourselves, all our
relationships will be peaceful. Is there a change
you need to make today?

. . . . .

World peace does depend on each one of us.
Have you considered what you might be willing
to do on its behalf? Today will offer some
unique opportunities.

. . . . .

Helping one person today helps all people.
We are not separate, one from another.
Our connection is there even
when we fail to see it.

Remember, wherever you are today, you have a job to do. Seek to see it. Then do it.

. . . . .

It is our work to love, to help, to forgive. Only when we practice these acts will we know peace. Today will offer opportunities.

. . . . .

Making a gratitude list, and then meditating on our blessings in the morning and before going to sleep, is a guaranteed way to feel peaceful. I will remember this practice today.

Taking a moment to reconsider a response can change the tenor of every conversation. I will take advantage of this exercise today.

. . . . .

Every one of us is an emissary for peace if we want to be. Every interaction any one of us has today is an opportunity that makes peace possible.

. . . . .

Every peace-filled moment manifests in kind. Will I demonstrate peace in my life today? That's the most important question facing me.

Always choosing peace rather than the need
to be right reduces tension. Besides, being right
is a matter of perspective. Being peaceful
is simply a choice. I will make the
right choice today.

. . . . .

Deciding to be peaceful feeds one's soul.
Arguing one's position doesn't.
Which will I choose today?

. . . . .

Every choice to be peaceful adds to the peace
of humankind. The impact any one of us has
on the world beyond our vision is far greater
than we can imagine. Let's do our
part for peace today.

A peaceful world requires peaceful people.
Can you be counted on today?

. . . . .

We are always in the right place at the right
time. This means, of course, that those we find
on our path are there intentionally too.
I will remember our need for
one another today.

. . . . .

Responding with kindness to anyone, anywhere
is never a mistake. It helps to change the world,
one person at a time. I will have many chances
to make a kind contribution today.

Today, let's commit to making every response
to everyone we encounter honorable.

. . . . .

The present as well as our future is determined
by each one of us. I will monitor my
actions carefully today.

. . . . .

How we experience each moment is "an inside
job." No one determines our perspective for us.
The empowerment that comes with this
understanding promises us as many
joyful days as we want.

Every single moment is sacred, never to be
repeated. Am I prepared to honor this
realization today?

. . . . .

Every experience offers us an opportunity to
extend peace to another person. Will I do my
part to make peace a reality today?

. . . . .

Every person we see today is playing a key role
in our lives. Do I fully appreciate this when I
look at the individuals crossing my path?

It is not only the love-filled people who deserve love in return. On the contrary, those who seem hardest to love deserve it even more. I will remember this today, person by person.

. . . . .

The past has no hold over us now. This present moment is all we have. It's where our lessons lie. Am I willing to be a good student today?

. . . . .

Surrendering is a choice for peace rather than tension. It changes the experience for everyone present. It doesn't mean our position was wrong, but that we chose freedom from its hold on us. Today might present an opportunity to practice this.

The sense of peace that comes over us when we
surrender, or simply walk away from an
argument, is intoxicating. And the
intoxication makes it easier the next time.
Try it today.

. . . . .

Simply being quiet may be one way of being
courteous. It may well be the easiest choice
you can practice today.

. . . . .

Using a soft voice makes being courteous easier.
For some, speaking softly may be a challenge.
Setting an example for others might be
your opportunity today.

Looking directly into the eyes of the person we
are talking to makes being kind an easier choice.
Have you noticed this? Do so today.

. . . . .

Do unto others as you want them to do unto
you. The Golden Rule is familiar to all of us.
But when did you last consciously
practice it? How about today?

. . . . .

One of the first things we were taught
as children was to be "nice." As adults,
we still need to remember this.
Will I need a reminder today?

Being courteous is a habit that takes practice.
And every day, the opportunities present
themselves. Keep track today of all the
times you succeed.

. . . . .

Deciding to be courteous takes the guesswork
out of every response. How much easier life
is when we have made this decision.
I will see the results today.

. . . . .

Being courteous will never come back to haunt
us. Being mean-spirited will. Today I can
make the choice I want.

Isolation closes the door to both human and conscious contact. Interacting with the messengers in our lives is the way we learn what we are here to learn. It doesn't happen in any other way.

. . . . .

Isolation will not protect us. Our "lessons" will wait. Being ready for one of them is a decision I can make today.

. . . . .

All injuries from our past must be forgiven. We cannot glimpse what the present is holding out to us if we have the past on our minds. And it's in the present where the gifts beckon to us.

Our level of peace is directly proportional
to our willingness to forgive past transgressions
against us. We don't need to be
prisoners of them any more. Today is
a new beginning.

. . . . .

Be kind. It's the right thing to do. And it takes no
forethought. Try it today, even once.

. . . . .

Be willing to be honorable. Kind.
Thoughtful and honest. The world and all
your relationships will reflect
your actions today.

Criticism never honors others, even when we
pretend we are being helpful. Setting a good
example for someone else does far more
than "suggesting" they change.
Give this idea a try today.

. . . . .

Smiling can help to heal an ugly situation.
It can also welcome a stranger into a room.
It's a far more powerful exercise
than words might be.

. . . . .

"Do no harm" is a simple, straightforward
admonition. It leaves no doubt about the right
action to take or the right words to say.
And following it can change every
moment of your day.

Our actions or words are either harmless
or they are not. This isn't mysterious.
It takes little more than attention to
our thoughts. Be vigilant today.

. . . . .

Any harm we do anywhere affects every person
alive, everywhere. This gives us an awesome
responsibility to do our best today.

. . . . .

Upon arising every morning, ask your
Higher Power for help to be kind.
Making the effort even once today will have
an impact on your mood.

Pause a moment before answering any question
or making any response today. In that moment,
remember kindness. Your life will
change accordingly.

. . . . .

Remember, being kind doesn't mean you have
to agree with what another person is saying
or doing today. It only means be kind!

. . . . .

We generally use a soft voice when we are being
kind. Let's practice this today.

. . . . .

Using hurtful words is never kind. Never!

Being kind means speaking from the heart.
If this is an unfamiliar practice, begin by
thinking loving thoughts before
speaking at all today.

. . . . .

Kindness isn't weakness. Never is it weakness.
It's generally one of the strongest measures
we can take. Try it today and see.

. . . . .

Kindness can transform a hateful situation and
a hateful person. Ourselves included. Do I
need to be transformed today?

Pray and Be Willing to Love VI

...

THERE ARE SO MANY WAYS for us to make a difference in another person's life. And not one of them takes very much effort or planning. One of the first and easiest ways that comes to mind is prayer. Saying a prayer for a friend or family member, with or without the person's knowledge, is a powerful act and one that will impact their lives, and ours, in a healing way.

A prayer for an adversary—an adversary of long duration or the person who angered you at the grocery or in traffic—is one of the most important prayers we can offer. If we commit to doing this, immediately for the casual adversary, or for thirty days for an enemy of longer term, our feelings will be changed, and we'll no longer feel the animosity that once held us hostage. The temper of the relationship will reflect our changed attitude too.

Praying for the ill and discouraged, those who feel helpless and hopeless, even if they are not aware you are praying for them, has beneficial results. Medical research has proven this to be the case. And every prayer that is said for one person, anywhere, any time, has an effect on everyone else too. Prayer knows no limits. It's like God in that way.

Even when we don't feel like praying for someone we know, or don't feel like holding loving thoughts of a colleague or neighbor or family member, if we keep our minds quiet and our hearts open, we will become aware of God's presence and will be guided to do the next right thing on behalf of whomever is in our midst. We don't have to do a lot of work, ever, to make a positive difference in the lives of the people who are sharing our journey at any moment in time.

We never have to be confused about God's will for our lives. It's always going to be gentle, loving, clear (if we are listening closely), and simple. Our lives are not meant to be complicated. Problems may arise, but solutions don't hide. God is always available to offer comfort and the way to peace. Let's seek God's direction in all things. Let's listen to God's message of hope. Let's be the carriers of

peace and kindness in all settings, among all grou
friends and strangers. Let's be aware that *who we bring*
any setting determines *who we find* there. If we want to
find love and peace and hope, we have to be an example
of it ourselves.

I have already referred to the expression of love and its
importance in other parts of this book, but it deserves
repeating. There is no more valuable contribution we can
make to our families, in our neighborhoods, at our places
of work, even in those places we visit only casually, than
thinking loving thoughts and expressing loving actions.

There are only two emotions: love and fear. Everyone
is demonstrating one or the other every minute of their
lives. And countering fear with love is the kindest response we can make. If we are attuned to God's message,
always a wise one, and quite often a quiet one, the choice
to do or say something loving will be easy and obvious.

The thoughts in this last part of this book will be helpful as reminders that we are in charge of the kind of life we
experience. If we want something different, we can create
it. If we rely on God's wisdom, pray, and have the willingness to listen and express love, today and every tomorrow
will be more than we could ever have imagined.

The *decision* to feel God's presence is all
that's needed to feel it. Now.

. . . . .

Listening is first a decision. And then an action.
Am I a good listener? Maybe today will be the
day I can practice this with gusto.

. . . . .

Listening becomes easier with practice, and the
messages we hear are often suggestions we
can incorporate, creating better lives.
Should I give this idea some
attention today?

If we listen intently to the person who has
captured our attention in the moment,
the response that is necessary will be clear.
Am I willing to be this attentive today?

. . . . .

Quietly listening fosters peace of mind,
provided that we aren't also listening to chatter
in our own minds. I will quiet the chatter today
not by denying it but by letting it go.

. . . . .

The messages we are now ready to hear for the
growth we are now ready to have are waiting for
our attention. Am I willing to listen today?

Listening to the person speaking is the clearest
and easiest way of honoring them. Do I do
this consistently, or do I need reminding?
I can practice this today and possibly
change another's life for the better.

. . . . .

Others have been ushered into our lives
intentionally. Honoring them by listening is
honoring God too. I can make some
improvements, no doubt. Today is
a good day to begin.

. . . . .

Prayer quiets our minds. In prayer,
I will hear God today.

Praying refreshes us. It educates us.
I want these gifts today. Do you?

. . . . .

Prayer has a way of changing every outcome.
It opens the door to God's involvement.
Today will become what it needs to be if
we stay out of God's way.

. . . . .

Prayer changes us. It makes us softer. It makes
us more trusting. It allows us to become more
willing to let God be in charge. Prayer is a good
daily practice. Don't forget it today.

Praying gives us something to do when we feel
lost and afraid. The gift in prayer is that we lose
our fear, because filling our minds with God
doesn't leave room for fear to take root.
Today I can be free of fear.

. . . . .

Prayer seems to change everyone in our lives,
but it's *we* who change. The result is the same,
however. The action is so simple and the gifts are
so great. Today is a day for praying.

. . . . .

Prayer has a power that is infinite. And there
are people—not coincidentally—around us
who are deserving of our prayers.
Let's pray on their behalf today.

Prayer will change the course of our history and
quite possibly the course of someone else's
history too. Let's put this in action today.

· · · · ·

Our journey is a series of learning partnerships
that "wear" our name. We will learn what
we need to learn more easily if prayer is one
of our tools. Was I willing to pray
upon arising today?

· · · · ·

We don't have to love our learning partners.
We simply have to acknowledge them and stay
open to the lessons being presented today.

Our experiences today have come calling
by design. They are important, but if we fail
to appreciate them, they will come again.

. . . . .

Every lesson, each experience is a building
block. Am I ready to lay the foundation today?

. . . . .

God is our partner through the process of every
lesson. If we don't hear the intended message,
it's only because we aren't listening. Am I
listening for God's message today?

Feeling love for any other person on our
path today changes how we ultimately feel
about everyone on our path.
The power of love is awesome.

· · · · ·

There are myriad times throughout the day
when silence might be the best response.
Am I willing to listen rather than have
the last word today?

· · · · ·

All struggles bring us closer to God if we allow
them to. In the process, it becomes possible
even to be grateful for the struggles.
Am I willing to consider this gift today?

No struggle can withstand the showering
of love. What a joy it is to melt away the tension
in our lives simply by responding with love
rather than anger. Perhaps today will offer
me the opportunity to practice.

. . . . .

Every potential argument can be an opportunity
for rejoicing if we are willing to practice
love and acceptance rather than
anger and rejection.

. . . . .

Willingness is up to me today.

Every difference of opinion today can be a
time for joining rather than an
experience of separation.

. . . . .

Every challenge contains within it the solution
if we can be open to it. Today may present
a challenge with which I can practice.

. . . . .

Being gentle means letting one's heart
be involved in the responses our partners
are waiting on. Am I willing
to be gentle today?

Being gentle never requires that we agree with
our adversaries. It simply means not being
mean. This is a decision I can make today.

. . . . .

Being gentle means letting your Higher Power
have a stake in your responses to others.
Today will be as peaceful as I allow it to be.

. . . . .

Gentleness changes everything about the
dynamics of a situation. It's an exercise that
empowers us while softening us, along
with those who are sharing the experience.
I will notice the power of
gentleness today.

When we let a relationship fester, we are
contributing to the chaotic world that
surrounds us. I will work to heal
a relationship today.

. . . . .

Healing ourselves or one another is everyone's
job. It begins with one tiny decision followed
by one tiny act of love. I will make
this decision today.

. . . . .

Willingness to listen and then follow one's inner
voice will save us from dishonest behavior,
which in turn will help us avoid the strife
that ultimately endangers all of us.
I will listen closely today.

Honesty is a decision. Not always an easy one,
however. But practice makes it second nature,
and that makes it possible for us to contribute
to the peace of the world, a worthy
contribution today.

. . . . .

Every time we treat another person with loving
honesty, we change them and ourselves too.
I will take advantage of an opportunity
to do this today.

. . . . .

Seeking God's direction in all things will ensure
that we respond to all our relationships both
honestly and humbly, thus making the world
a more peaceful place today.

Before taking any action, take a minute to seek
God's help and perspective. The results will
astound you. It can become a habit with enough
practice. Today can be the first day
of a new outlook.

. . . . .

Experiencing gratitude can become a habit, one
that will change your life. Begin the habit today.

. . . . .

Any attitude will become a habit with practice.
Be wary of negative attitudes. If one creeps
up today, ask your Higher Power for
a new perspective.

Making a gratitude list every day is an excellent way of changing our minds, thus our lives. Today is the right day for noticing the good.

. . . . .

Any day you aren't feeling content, reread yesterday's gratitude list. This practice will change your perspective. Today is as good as we decide to make it.

. . . . .

Upon arising, think first of God. What a simple suggestion. What a profound result it promises. Try it tomorrow, since today is already underway.

As you ponder any thought or action, try to discern what God would have you think or do. Will you adhere to this suggestion all day?

. . . . .

Make a habit of taking God with you wherever you go. God is a great companion, and the day's activities are guaranteed to be more peaceful. I will seek to enjoy God's presence all day.

. . . . .

Conversing with God is only as hard as we make it. God is a great listener. But are we? I will try to listen to God's suggestions today.

While doing any task, complex or simple,
be aware of God's presence. It will make the
work easier. Today's tasks will be easy
if I remember God.

. . . . .

Remember, God never leaves. It's our minds
that lose their focus. I will keep my mind
where it belongs today. On God.

. . . . .

If we are experiencing any anxiety, we have
forgotten to remember God's presence.
Today will be as free from anxiety
as my memory allows.

What we need to know and experience will
surface. Always. I will be ready for my lessons
today. I will ask God to be my companion too.

. . . . .

Love is always the right expression in any
situation. It's the response that diffuses conflict.
It's the response that heals hurt and confusion.
It's also what God is giving me today
and every day.

. . . . .

Love is more easily recognized than fear,
because fear wears many faces. But the proper
response to all experiences is love.
It's the response God would want
me to make today.

A loving response in any situation is the right
response, even when it's hard to do.
Relying on God for help makes it
easier, however.

. . . . .

Everyone is looking for love regardless of what
their behavior suggests. Knowing this
makes our proper response obvious,
doesn't it? Am I willing to do
the obvious thing today?

. . . . .

We can shift from feeling fear to feeling love
instantly. It's a decision that gets easier with
time and practice and help from God.
Am I seeking the help I need today?

Every loving expression we offer comes back
to us. So does every other expression.
Am I seeking love today?
There is a way to get it.

. . . . .

Feelings have only the power we give them.
We are in charge of our feelings. Not the other
way around. Will I remember this today?

. . . . .

Every word we say (or think) is heard by God.
Are we comfortable with our inner dialogue as
well as our conversations with others? I will
remember that God is listening to
my conversations today.

We will be grateful for every moment of the
journey in due time. Today's experiences will be
appreciated. That's a guarantee.

. . . . .

What is true now and always will be true is this:
Every person and every experience is holy.
I pray to remember this today, especially
if I am feeling agitated.

. . . . .

Even the angry person on our path has a lesson
for us, deserves our recognition and then our
blessing. This understanding will
simplify my life today.

Cherish both the good and the bad of the past.
One was not more valuable than the other.
All experiences were what we needed to
get *here, now.* The same will be true
of today's experiences.

. . . . .

"Coincidences" are really by design. Nothing is
accidental. There are no chance encounters
or situations. There is relief in this awareness
if we choose to see it that way. Today is
full of promise, isn't it?

Walking away from any situation that causes you
unrest gives you a fresh perspective on every
other tense situation too. We don't have
to be drawn into conflict, ever.
I can practice this today.

. . . . .

This world would look very different if more
of us were willing to surrender our position
on anything. *Choosing peace instead of this*
is a wonderfully freeing option.
Why not try it today?

. . . . .

Choosing peace rather than conflict is a small
decision whose time has come.
Why not demonstrate this
in your own life today?

Agreeing to disagree is one way of choosing
peace. It's easier than full surrender but
just as effective. There may well be
opportunities to do this today.

· · · · ·

Courtesy is one way of expressing love.
And it takes no planning. Only willingness.
I can be courteous today.

· · · · ·

Being courteous today simply makes sense.
All of us will benefit.

Being alone too long with our thoughts is
seldom beneficial. The input of others is what's
intended. We are sharing the journey with our
teachers. Listen to them today.

. . . . .

Isolation and meditation are not the same thing.
Isolation is avoidance and is generally painful.
Meditation suggests willingness to listen
to the guidance of our Higher Power.
Today is open. What's your choice?

. . . . .

Harboring any resentment prevents any peace.
Taking an inventory of what we are holding
onto is a necessary step to finding the
peace we deserve. Today will be an
opportunity for a fresh start.

Don't disparage another person. Ever.
The repercussions are endless. If peace is what
we want—and who doesn't?—we have one
obvious way to find it. Express it.
Today can be a beginning.

· · · · ·

Pause, think, and seek guidance before
responding in any situation. This will prevent
harm, and it will promote peace. Can I be
a peacemaker today?

· · · · ·

There are many ways to honor others. Prayer
honors. Loving thoughts honor. Listening
honors. I am capable of doing at least one
of these today. The world will be
the better for it too.

Love is often best expressed by detachment.
We must let others have their own journey.
I can practice this today.

. . . . .

Detachment doesn't mean I can't pray
for someone today.

. . . . .

Remember that God is waiting for your request
for help in all matters, all decisions,
all conversations today.

To Our Readers

. . .

CONARI PRESS, an imprint of Red Wheel/Weiser, publishes books on topics ranging from spirituality, personal growth, and relationships to women's issues, parenting, and social issues. Our mission is to publish quality books that will make a difference in people's lives—how we feel about ourselves and how we relate to one another. We value integrity, compassion, and receptivity, both in the books we publish and in the way we do business.

. . . . .

Our readers are our most important resource, and we value your input, suggestions, and ideas about what you would like to see published. Please feel free to contact us, to request our latest book catalog, or to be added to our mailing list.

Conari Press
An imprint of Red Wheel/Weiser, LLC
P.O. Box 612
York Beach, ME 03910-0612

. . . . .

www.conari.com